Yesterday & Today

HOMES

Joanne Mattern

BLACKBIRCH®
PRESS

THOMSON
GALE

San Diego • Detroit • New York • San Francisco • Cleveland • New Haven, Conn. • Waterville, Maine • London • Munich

THOMSON
GALE

Picture Credits
Cover: Art Today, Inc. (both)
© Archivo Iconografico, S.A./CORBIS, 7, 11
© Art Today, Inc., 25 (inset), 31 (both)
© Bettmann/CORBIS, 4, 22 (bottom), 27 (inset), 28
© Burstein Collection/CORBIS, 10
© COREL Corporation, 14, 25
© Dore/Dover Publications, 17, 19
© Ric Ergenbright/CORBIS, 21
© Fine Art Photographic Library, London/Art Resource, NY, 23
© Michael Freeman/CORBIS, 30 (both)
© Historical Picture Archive/CORBIS, 20

© Hulton-Deutsch Collection/CORBIS, 12
© Hanan Isachar/CORBIS, 29
© Erich Lessing/Art Resource, Inc., 18
© Ludovic Maisant/CORBIS, 13 (top)
© Mary Evans Picture Library, 5
© National Archives, 26
© New York Historical Society, 27 (right)
© North Wind Picture Archives, 6 (inset), 8, 9 (both), 22 (top), 24
© Photo Disc, Inc., 16 (both)
© Carl & Ann Purcell/CORBIS, 15
© Stapleton Collection/CORBIS, 6 (top)
© Tim Thomson/CORBIS, 13 (inset)

LIBRARY OF CONGRESS CATALOGING-IN-PUBLICATION DATA

Mattern, Joanne, 1963–
  Homes / by Joanne Mattern.
    p. cm. — (Yesterday and today)
  Includes bibliographical references and index.
  ISBN 1-4103-0425-6 (hardback: alk. paper)
  1. Dwellings, History. I. Title. II. Series.

  TH4808.M38 2004
  728–dc22

                                                        2004008270

Table of Contents

Homes During Prehistoric Times

People who live in different parts of the world build different kinds of houses. Climate helps determine what kind of home is needed. People who live in cold, snowy climates need houses that hold heat in and keep cold and snow out. People who live in wet climates need houses that keep out rain.

Another important factor in home construction is what materials are available. During early times, it was very difficult to move material from one place to another. People used what was nearby. For example, people who lived near forests used wood to build houses.

The first humans hunted animals and gathered plants to eat. They moved from place to place in search of food. Some lived in caves. Others built simple huts out of mud and grass. These huts provided shelter from

Because they had to move from place to place to find food, prehistoric people lived in temporary housing, such as simple mud and grass huts or caves.

4

Once people began to plant crops and raise animals for food, they built more permanent homes and villages.

Prehistory

500 B.C.

100 B.C.

A.D. 100

200

500

1000

1200

1300

1400

1500

1600

1700

1800

1900

2000

2100

cold, wind, and rain. They also protected people from wild animals. Mud and grass huts could be built quickly and abandoned when it was time to move on.

Animal hides were another source of shelter. People in ancient Europe stretched reindeer hides over poles to create tepees. A hole at the top of the tepee let out smoke from the fire they used for heat and cooking. The tepees could be folded up and carried.

About eleven thousand years ago, people began to plant crops and raise cattle, sheep, and other animals. Now they could live in one place. This meant that houses could be more permanent.

People in Europe and Asia built huts out of sticks tied together with reeds and covered with clay to keep out the rain, snow, and wind. These homes were supported by strong wooden poles and had straw roofs. Huts were built close together to create villages.

Ancient Egyptians lived along the Nile River and built their homes from the reeds, clay, limestone, and granite they found near the river.

Ancient Egypt and the Middle East

People who lived in the Middle East about five thousand years ago used different materials to build their homes than people who lived in Europe and northern Asia. Many Egyptians lived along the banks of the Nile River. There was a good supply of clay along the river. The hills around the river provided different types of rocks, such as limestone and granite. These rocks and the clay were good materials with which to build houses.

To build a house, people dug a hole to make the house's foundation. A foundation is the base on which a house is built. Next, people formed clay into bricks. Then they set the bricks out in the sun to dry. The bricks were stacked up and stuck together with a mixture of sand, lime, and water called mortar.

The use of mud bricks changed the shape of houses. Until then, most Middle Eastern houses were round. Since bricks are rectangular, people built square or rectangular houses.

A typical Egyptian house was about thirty feet long by ten feet wide. The roof was flat and sometimes had a hole in it so people could climb outside to use the roof as extra living space. Each house had its own door. The first room was a public room, where the family entertained visitors. Another public room held a shrine to the gods. Behind these rooms were private bedrooms for the family. A kitchen was at the back of the house. Underneath the house was a cellar that was used for storage. Houses had few windows. The lack of windows and the thick walls kept out the heat.

Crowded Town

The Middle Eastern town of Çatalhüyük had no streets. Instead, the houses were built next to each other, and each house shared a wall with the house next door. The houses were so close together that the inhabitants could not go in and out through a front door. Instead, residents climbed over the flat roofs and down a ladder into their house.

Prehistory ——

500 B.C. ——

100 B.C. ——

A.D. 100 ——

200 ——

500 ——

1000 ——

1200 ——

1300 ——

1400 ——

1500 ——

1600 ——

1700 ——

1800 ——

1900 ——

2000 ——

2100 ——

Çatalhüyük's residents entered their homes through the roof because they did not have front doors.

Ancient Greece and Rome

Look Out Below!

Insulae had no drains or places to get rid of garbage. The inhabitants simply threw garbage and waste material out of the window and onto the street below.

Like the people of the Middle East, those who lived in Greece and Rome two thousand years ago discovered new ways to build houses. Because Rome and Greece have hot climates, it was important that houses provide cool shelters that allowed a lot of air to flow through them. To achieve this goal, houses were built around open spaces called courtyards. These courtyards let light and air into the inner rooms. They also were places for people to meet and talk with their friends.

Greek houses were built of brick or stone. The bricks and stones were held together with mortar. The roofs were made of tile. Several rooms were arranged around the central courtyard. Some were used as bedrooms. Others were workrooms, where people made pottery or worked on other crafts. There were also a kitchen, pantry, and storage areas.

In most cultures, the type of house people live in is based on how rich they are. In ancient Rome, rich

Wealthy Romans lived in villas, which had many rooms all surrounding a central courtyard.

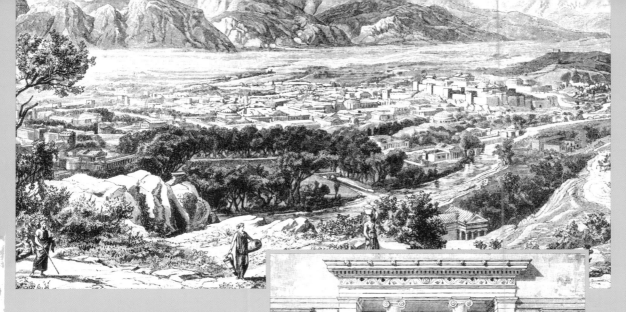

Prehistory

500 B.C.

100 B.C.

A.D. 100

200

500

1000

1200

1300

1400

1500

1600

1700

1800

1900

2000

2100

people lived in large buildings called villas. Villas were made of brick or stone. They had only one floor, but they had many rooms. These rooms included bedrooms, workshops, and a kitchen. The most important part of the kitchen was the hearth, or fireplace. The hearth was used to cook food. Roman villas even had running water for drinking, washing, and carrying away human waste. They had central heating, too. Hot water flowed through pipes under the floor to heat the rooms. As in ancient Greece, the rooms in Roman villas were arranged around a central courtyard that provided light and air.

Conditions were very different for Rome's poor citizens. Poor people lived in apartment houses called *insulae*. An *insula* could have up to four or five floors. There was no running water or sanitation. Rooms were small and crowded. The lower floors of the *insulae* were made of bricks held together with mortar. The upper floors were built of wood and plaster. Because the builders used poor quality materials, the *insulae* often collapsed. Other *insulae* caught fire when the residents' wood-burning stoves ignited the wood and plaster. Many Romans were killed in *insulae* disasters.

In the flourishing cities of ancient Greece (top), imposing columns and decorative elements often adorned the homes of wealthy citizens (shown).

Ancient China

While people were building with wood in Europe and mud bricks in the Middle East, people in China built their own style of houses.

Farmers usually built their homes from mud bricks with reed or tile roofs. The foundations of these simple houses were often below the ground. This kept the family warmer in the winter and cooler in the summer. Other Chinese houses were made of wood or bamboo. Most Chinese people preferred wood because they liked the way it looked. Also, wood was lighter and less likely to injure people if the house collapsed in an earthquake.

Upper-class Chinese people lived in courtyard houses. Courtyard houses showed the importance of beauty and harmony in Chinese design. They featured rows of buildings arranged in a square around an inner courtyard. The inner courtyard had trees, paths, and small gardens. It was a quiet, beautiful place. Covered walkways connected the buildings. Another courtyard surrounded the back of the buildings. Everything was enclosed by a high wall. Rich, important families had more buildings arranged in more squares to create multiple courtyards. The more important a family was, the more courtyards and buildings the home had.

Courtyard homes usually did not have indoor kitchens. Instead, food was cooked and prepared outside. Basins of water were brought inside for

In China, farmers and common people lived in simple homes with thatched roofs.

The homes of upper-class people often had many buildings surrounding an inner courtyard.

Prehistory

500 B.C.

100 B.C.

A.D. 100

200

500

1000

1200

1300

1400

1500

1600

1700

1800

1900

2000

2100

washing. An outdoor toilet was in a corner of the outer courtyard.

Homes in China were carefully designed for balance. If a line was drawn down the center of the courtyard, all the buildings on one side would be arranged exactly the same way as the buildings on the other.

Keeping Evil Out

A wall was always located across from the entrance to a courtyard house. This design was intended to stop evil spirits from entering the house. It was believed these spirits could not turn corners. In addition, a high step at the entrance was thought to keep out evil spirits.

Premedieval Times

Society changed a great deal in Europe during the first one thousand years A.D. The Roman Empire fell, and its villas, with heat and running water, disappeared. Instead, different tribes ruled parts of Europe. Most people lived as poor peasants who worked for powerful lords.

Peasants built their homes out of whatever materials they could find. Pieces of wood, dried mud, and stone were common building materials. The roofs were made of thatch, which is a mixture of straw and reeds. Peasant houses usually had just one room. People ate and slept in this room. Often, their pigs, cows, or other animals lived in the house with them. Animals were kept inside because there was not enough land or building materials for peasants to build a separate barn.

Lords lived in larger homes called halls. Halls were made of tall, straight pieces of timber connected with a mixture of woven twigs covered with clay, called wattle and daub. Often, a hall contained one large room. The lord's soldiers ate and drank in that room. At night, they slept there on woven mats that were stored against the walls during the day. The lord and his family might have their own living quarters in a separate room, but spent a lot of their time in the main room with the others.

The Vikings of Scandinavia also lived in halls. Their homes were called longhouses. The Vikings used

European peasants built their one-room homes from wood, dried mud, and stone, and covered the roof with straw and reeds.

Prehistory ——

500 B.C. ——

100 B.C. ——

A.D. 100 ——

200 ——

500 ——

1000 ——

1200 ——

1300 ——

1400 ——

1500 ——

1600 ——

1700 ——

1800 ——

1900 ——

2000 ——

2100 ——

The Vikings used wooden tiles instead of thatch for their roofs when they built their longhouses (above). They divided the inside of their homes into small rooms (left) and used very little furniture.

wooden tiles on their roofs instead of thatch. They also used nails instead of wooden pegs. A Viking longhouse was divided into several smaller rooms. These rooms were used for different purposes, such as sleeping, cooking, eating, and working. Viking homes did not have much furniture. There were a few stools to sit on. People slept on quilts placed on wooden platforms along the wall.

Food was stored in barrels. The stove was a small fire surrounded by rocks to keep people and animals away from the flames.

A Sunny View

The Anglo-Saxons ruled England from the 400s until 1066. Anglo-Saxon houses were often built facing south to allow the sun's light and warmth to come through the doors and windows. During bad weather, the windows were covered with shutters to keep out rain, snow, and cold.

The Maya in Central America

Houses in Central America were very different from those in Europe or China. Between A.D. 300 and A.D. 900, the Maya lived in Central America, in what is now Mexico.

Most Maya were farmers. They lived in small villages scattered through the jungle. Like most people, the Maya used local materials to build their homes. Jungle homes had wooden planks for the walls. The roofs were made of palm leaves tied to a wooden frame. These roofs were very steep to keep off the rain.

Some Maya lived in the mountains. Because there were few trees here, these people used stones stuck together with mortar to build their homes. Mountain homes often had thatched roofs made of grass or straw.

The Maya who lived in the mountains of Mexico built their homes with stone and mortar, similar to this Mayan temple.

Prehistory —
500 B.C. —
100 B.C. —
A.D. 100 —
200 —
500 —
1000 —
1200 —
1300 —
1400 —
1500 —
1600 —
1700 —
1800 —
1900 —
2000 —
2100 —

Mayan farmers, who lived in the jungle, built their huts with very steep roofs made of palm leaves to keep the rain out. They often slept in one hut and cooked and ate in a separate one nearby.

A Mayan house could be round, square, or rectangular. The shape depended on what the house was made of. A wall inside the house divided it into two rooms. One room was used for sleeping, and the other was for cooking and eating. Some families had two houses on a small piece of land. One house was used for cooking and eating. The other was used for sleeping.

The central feature of the cooking room or house was the hearth. This was usually made of three large stones that surrounded an open fire. Smoke from the fire escaped through a hole cut in the roof.

Mayan houses did not have running water. If there were no rivers or other bodies of water nearby, the Maya got their water from a well near the house.

The Maya did not spend much time inside their homes. They spent most of the day farming or working outside. To them, home was just a place to eat and sleep.

FAST FACT

The Maya believed it was important to keep the spirits of their ancestors nearby. So they buried their dead under the floors of their houses.

Castles in Medieval Europe

The period between A.D. 500 and A.D. 1500 is known as the European Middle Ages. During this time, outlaws and armies threatened people throughout the continent. Lords needed larger, more secure homes to protect themselves and the peasants who supported them. They began to build large, strong buildings called castles.

Castles were built of stone instead of wood. Stone was much stronger and easier to defend, because it does not burn. Castles were usually built in places that were hard to attack, such as on mountains or along lakes or rivers.

Castles were surrounded by one or more high stone walls. Watchtowers on top of the walls provided places where soldiers could watch for the enemy. Sometimes a castle was surrounded by a deep pit of water called a moat.

Because castles were intended to be fortresses rather than homes, they were not very

During the Middle Ages, lords built strong stone castles with high walls and watchtowers (above) or moats (right) to protect themselves from outlaws and foreign armies.

Castles were large enough to house a lord's family members as well as his servants. When the castle became too dirty, however, the nobility left for another one while servants cleaned up after them.

Prehistory —

500 B.C. —

100 B.C. —

A.D. 100 —

200 —

500 —

1000 —

1200 —

1300 —

1400 —

1500 —

1600 —

1700 —

1800 —

1900 —

2000 —

2100 —

comfortable places in which to live. The thick stone walls made them cold, and the long hallways and big rooms were drafty. Residents hung tapestries on the walls. They lined the stone floors with dried grass and reeds to make the rooms warmer. When the reeds got dirty, they were thrown out and replaced with fresh, clean ones.

Most castles had a central hall that was used for banquets and special ceremonies. There were separate bedrooms for family members. Servants had their own living quarters. People slept on mattresses stuffed with straw. Large, sunny rooms called solariums were used by the women. They needed light to sew clothes and tapestries. Kitchens were located on the lower floor, or sometimes in a separate wing. These kitchens included a large fireplace where food was prepared.

Castle Bathrooms

A bathroom in a castle was a seat over a hollow space inside the walls. When a person used the bathroom, the waste flowed down to a cesspit below the castle. After a while, the castle and the cesspit smelled so bad that the inhabitants would move to another castle while servants cleaned up the mess.

The Rise of the Middle Class

Before A.D. 1000, Europeans were usually either peasants or royalty. After A.D. 1000, however, a new social class emerged in Europe. People in this new middle class generally worked as merchants or craftspeople. They had more money than the peasants, so they could build better houses.

Middle-class houses were usually built of timber. Oak was the most common building material because it was very strong. Oak trees were chopped down and cut into long sections. Then the timbers were brought to the building site and put together. Wooden pegs held the pieces together. The timbers did not fit tightly together, so builders filled the spaces between them with stones, plaster, smaller pieces of wood, or wattle and daub. The house was usually shaped like a large box and had only one story. It was divided into bedrooms, a living room, and a dining room. The floors were made of wood. Most people covered the windows with shutters. Only the rich could afford to have glass windows.

In larger cities and towns, merchants and craftsmen often had their shops next to, or even, in their homes.

In the cities, there was not enough space to build large, separate houses. Instead, middle-class city dwellers often lived in town houses. A town house is a large, two- or three-story single-family home that shares a common wall with the house next door. Town houses were built in rows and were several stories high. The merchant's shop was often on the first floor. Storage space and living quarters were on the floors above.

Medieval houses did not have running water or working toilets. Some houses had outside toilets. Others had special rooms called garderobes. A garderobe was a bathroom that was built on the outside of the house, near the roof. It had a seat with a hole in it that allowed waste to drop to the ground below.

FAST FACT

Kitchens in medieval houses were often located in a separate building to reduce the risk of fire. This was especially important when many wooden buildings were crowded into a small space.

With the rise of a middle class in Europe, people began to build stronger houses made of oak logs.

Prehistory

500 B.C.

100 B.C.

A.D. 100

200

500

1000

1200

1300

1400

1500

1600

1700

1800

1900

2000

2100

A Change in Style

During the 1500s, Europe experienced an explosion of art and culture. As art became fancier and more elaborate, so did many homes.

Wealthy Europeans began to build houses that were like palaces. These houses were several stories high and had many large rooms. Usually, the upper floors included bedrooms, sitting rooms, and other living areas for the family. The first floor included a large dining room and space to entertain guests or hold concerts and other entertainment. The servants' quarters were located in the

During the 1500s, people in Europe and China (below) began to build bigger, more elaborate homes.

basement. Here an assortment of staff members lived and worked. Servants included maids, cooks, housekeepers, gardeners, and cleaners. It took a lot of people to run a large house.

European houses were elaborately decorated during this time. They often had carved figures of angels or animals on the outside. Doors were bordered by carved archways featuring artistic designs.

Until the 1600s, most European houses were made of wood. Then people began to use bricks. This was an important change because bricks would not burn, so they were much safer than wood. Brick houses also looked much different than houses built with wood. In the crowded cities, rows of brick houses looked very much alike.

Europe was not the only part of the world that had crowded cities. In Asia, people were also jammed into cities and trying to find places to live. In Beijing, China, residents crammed into neighborhoods called *hutongs*. *Hutongs* were small wood and tile houses squeezed into narrow lanes. Many families lived in a small group of rooms, with one or two rooms for each family. *Hutongs* often had colorful names, such as The Lane of the Arrow Makers, or The Alley of the Houses Decorated by Arched Gateways.

Plenty of Room

Royal palaces were especially large. In 1519, King Francis I of France began to build a hunting lodge named Chambord. Chambord has 440 rooms, 365 fireplaces, and more than 80 staircases. Unfortunately, the house was so cold and uncomfortable that Francis only stayed there for a few days at a time.

Although Chambord had 440 rooms and 365 fireplaces, it was so cold and uncomfortable the king never stayed long.

Prehistory ——

500 B.C. ——

100 B.C. ——

A.D. 100 ——

200 ——

500 ——

1000 ——

1200 ——

1300 ——

1400 ——

1500 ——

1600 ——

1700 ——

1800 ——

1900 ——

2000 ——

2100 ——

The Industrial Revolution

During the late 1700s, Europe and America were transformed by the Industrial Revolution. During this time, machines made it possible to mass-produce items that had once been made by hand. Factories and mills began to produce everything from clothing to soap. Thousands of people moved into cities to work in these new factories.

Factory owners often built houses for their workers. To save money and fit the largest number of people into the smallest amount of space, many factory owners built row houses for their employees. Row houses were small, narrow, wooden houses that shared a common wall on either side. These houses often had few rooms or modern conveniences.

During the Industrial Revolution, many people moved from their farms to the cities to work in factories and textile mills (top). Factory workers were often forced to live in slums (above).

Other workers lived in one or two rooms in larger apartment buildings. An apartment building includes many smaller living units, or sets of rooms. These buildings were often crowded, dirty, dangerous, and poorly built. These neighborhoods were called slums.

During the 1800s, some workers built houses outside the city, then took a train into the city to work. These new areas were called suburbs. Houses in the suburbs were often small and simple. They were made of brick or wood. Each house had its own garden or small yard.

Wealthy people built large houses in the countryside. In Great Britain, the years between 1837 and 1901 were called the Victorian era. Queen Victoria ruled the nation at that time. Victorian houses were large and carefully decorated with towers and painted trim. Inside, these homes usually included rooms called parlors—where the inhabitants entertained guests—many bedrooms, libraries, and playrooms for the children.

During the late 1800s, houses began to include exciting new features, such as central heating and indoor plumbing. They also had gas or electric lights, running water, and telephone service.

While the working classes found themselves living in slums, wealthy people lived in large, beautifully decorated homes in the countryside.

Prehistory

500 B.C.

100 B.C.

A.D. 100

200

500

1000

1200

1300

1400

1500

1600

1700

1800

1900

2000

2100

The American Frontier

Mud-Brick Homes

Native Americans and Hispanic settlers in the western part of the United States had long built their homes out of sun-dried mud and straw bricks called adobe. These structures are so strong that some have been standing for hundreds of years.

Pioneers who settled the American West during the 1800s built log cabins.

Beginning in the 1600s, Europeans began settling in North America. By the 1800s, several million people were living throughout the United States and Canada. Eastern areas were settled first. Then pioneers headed west in large numbers in search of land and a new way of life.

Eastern cities and towns looked a lot like cities and towns in Europe. Many houses were built of wood. Later, brick houses became common as well. Many houses had front porches where people could sit or entertain visitors.

Pioneers who settled in areas with lots of trees often built log cabins. This type of house was originally built in Scandinavia and Germany. Immigrants from these countries brought the style to America. Logs were notched, or cut, at the ends and then stacked to fit together. The spaces between the logs were filled with twigs and clay. Log cabins were usually small and had just one or two rooms. The main room was used for cooking, eating, and sometimes sleeping. Sometimes

Prehistory —

500 B.C. —

100 B.C. —

A.D. 100 —

200 —

500 —

1000 —

1200 —

1300 —

1400 —

1500 —

1600 —

1700 —

1800 —

1900 —

2000 —

2100 —

smaller bedrooms were located behind the main room or upstairs in the attic. The door was an animal skin or a rough plank of wood. A latch and string through a hole in the door served as a lock. Because glass was very expensive and difficult to carry or ship to the West, windows were covered with oiled paper to keep out wind, rain, and insects.

Settlers on the prairies of the Midwest could not build log cabins because these areas had few trees. Instead, many settlers built dugouts. These homes were dug out of the ground. The sides were lined with rocks or tree branches. Layers of hay or sod were placed over more branches to make a roof.

Living underground was unpleasant. The dugouts often became infested with insects, and sometimes the walls and roof leaked in the rain. Most settlers built wooden houses as soon as they had the money to buy and ship timber from the East.

Some of the adobe-brick (inset) homes that Native Americans built hundreds of years ago were so strong that they are still standing today.

Crowded Cities in the Twentieth Century

More and more people moved into cities during the twentieth century. There was little room for single-family houses in crowded American or European cities. Instead, people crowded into apartment buildings. These large buildings were divided into smaller living units in order to house a lot of people in a relatively small amount of space.

Some apartment buildings were poorly built and did not provide a healthy, safe place in which to live. Every large city had slums filled with these tenements. These buildings were often built so close together that the rooms received little fresh air. The rooms of an apartment were sometimes located one behind the other. This meant that only the rooms at each end would have a window. Many people shared one or two small bedrooms. Often, many children would sleep in the same bed. The apartments also included a tiny kitchen and living room.

Sanitation facilities were also poor in many tenements. Residents on each floor usually shared one bathroom or toilet. Because there was little room inside the apartments, residents often sat outside on the front steps to visit with each other and enjoy some fresh air and sunlight. Children played in the streets and alleyways.

In time, cement and steel began to replace wood and brick as building materials. These materials were inexpensive and easy to make. After the electric elevator was invented in 1880, buildings

Tenement buildings were built so close together that children living in them had no place to play but in the streets and alleyways.

became taller. These tall buildings became known as high-rises.

Modern high-rise apartment buildings were more comfortable than tenements. Most had running water and bathrooms for each apartment, along with heat, electric light, and fans or air conditioners to circulate fresh air. Wealthy residents could afford especially fancy apartments. These could have several floors, a rooftop garden, and large rooms with spectacular views through big windows.

Going Up

Some city apartment buildings have penthouse apartments on the top floor. Penthouses are usually very large and expensive. These apartments can be bigger than a small suburban house.

After the invention of the elevator (above), people began to build high-rise apartment buildings that offered more comfortable housing for city dwellers.

Prehistory

500 B.C.

100 B.C.

A.D. 100

200

500

1000

1200

1300

1400

1500

1600

1700

1800

1900

2000

2100

Mass Production

Until the middle of the 1900s, most houses were built one at a time. After World War II ended in 1945, builders began to mass-produce houses and building materials such as walls, roofs, and windows. This allowed houses to be built quickly and cheaply, which made them available to more people. Soon, communities in North America, Europe, and Australia were filled with these new houses.

In the United States, soldiers returning from World War II were eager to move into new homes with their growing families. In 1946, two thousand homes were built on Long Island, New York. This planned community became known as Levittown, after its builder, William Levitt. Levittown houses all looked alike. Each house had a living room, kitchen, two bedrooms, and one bathroom on the first floor. The second floor was an attic that could be made into more bedrooms. These houses measured about seven

Using mass production, thousands of low-cost homes, all exactly alike, were built in Levittown, New York, for soldiers returning from World War II.

hundred square feet and sold for $7,000, which equaled about $66,000 in 2003.

During the next thirty years, housing developments were built all over America. Housing styles varied. The ranch was a one-floor house. The bi-level or high-ranch was a ranch house with a finished basement that provided a second level of living space. The colonial was a larger, traditional style. It featured a kitchen, dining room, and living room on the first floor and bedrooms and bathrooms upstairs. Housing developments allowed thousands of families to achieve the dream of owning their own homes.

While modern, mass-produced styles became common in North America, Europe, and Australia, other parts of the world continued to use traditional styles and building practices. Families in rural parts of South America, Asia, and Africa still build and live in traditional houses made from local materials such as reeds, grass, and mud. At the same time, cities on these continents usually feature high-rise apartment buildings, just like cities in Europe and North America.

Hundreds of small concrete moshav houses were built for the settlers of the newly formed state of Israel in 1948.

Israel's Moshav Houses

When the state of Israel was founded in 1948, hundreds of thousands of people settled there. Many settled in communities called moshavim. *Moshavim* is the Hebrew word for "homes." To handle the overwhelming demand for housing, builders created special moshav houses. These houses were made of concrete poured over a steel frame. These small houses included a kitchen, bathroom, and two bedrooms. Later, families added more rooms.

Prehistory ——

500 B.C. ——

100 B.C. ——

A.D. 100 ——

200 ——

500 ——

1000 ——

1200 ——

1300 ——

1400 ——

1500 ——

1600 ——

1700 ——

1800 ——

1900 ——

2000 ——

2100 ——

Today, homes are built in many shapes, sizes, and designs. Many combine a variety of building materials, including wood, stone, brick, steel, concrete, and even plastic.

Homes Today

Today, there are a variety of different types of houses in Europe and North America. Most are made of wood, while others are made of brick or stone. Houses generally follow traditional designs, although they have gotten much larger over the years.

Wood, brick, and stone are not the only materials used to build today's houses. Some houses are built of steel or concrete. Plastic is used more and more in home construction. Today's houses often have plastic pipes instead of the copper pipes used in earlier times.

Today's homes are much more energy efficient than homes built thirty or more years ago. Most homes in colder climates

Solar Power

Solar energy can be collected in solar cells made of an element called silicon. One solar cell that is four inches in diameter can produce one watt of electric power. The more solar cells, the more power can be collected. This power can be used right away or stored in batteries.

are tightly insulated to keep cold air out and warm air in. Appliances and heating systems use less energy than older models. Some homes have solar panels to collect the sun's power and change it into energy to run appliances and heat the house.

Modern houses have also become increasingly electronic. Electric appliances are now used to handle routine tasks, such as washing dishes, cooking food, and doing laundry. Home entertainment systems feature movie-quality sound systems, big-screen televisions, and DVD players. Computers are wired to each other and the outside world. New houses must contain special wiring and extra electrical outlets to handle these high-tech appliances.

Modern technology is sure to touch traditional homes in other areas of the world as well. In Asia and Africa, more and more people are leaving their traditional homes in the countryside and moving into high-rise apartment buildings in the city. These moves have a dramatic effect on people's lives and society itself.

Homes have changed a great deal over the centuries, but one thing has remained the same. From ancient huts to modern high-rises, from traditional styles to high-tech marvels, people have always tried to make their homes into welcoming places in which to live.

Some homes use solar panels, which collect the sun's power in solar cells (inset) and convert it to energy to heat the house and run the appliances.

Prehistory ——

500 B.C. ——

100 B.C. ——

A.D. 100 ——

200 ——

500 ——

1000 ——

1200 ——

1300 ——

1400 ——

1500 ——

1600 ——

1700 ——

1800 ——

1900 ——

2000 ——

2100 ——

Glossary

archaeologists: Scientists who study the past by digging up old buildings and objects.

cesspit: A large hole where waste is collected.

clay: A kind of earth that can be shaped when wet.

climate: The usual weather in a place.

foundation: A hole dug beneath a house to form a base for construction.

hearth: A large fireplace.

mortar: A mixture of lime, sand, water, and cement that is used for building.

peasants: A class of people who work on farms.

sod: The top layer of soil and grass.

story: A floor or level in a building.

tenements: Run-down or poorly built apartment buildings.

thatch: Straw or reeds.

timber: Wood cut from trees and used for building.

wattle and daub: Woven twigs covered with clay.

For More Information

Books

Raymond Bial, *Building America: The Houses.* Tarrytown, NY: Benchmark Books, 2002.

Albert Lorenz, *House.* New York: Harry N. Abrams, 1998.

Bonnie Shemie, *Houses of China.* Toronto, Canada: Tundra Books, 1996.

Tim Woods, *Houses and Homes.* New York: Viking, 1997.

Web Sites

Houses and Homes (www.schools.ash.org.auelanorah/homes. html). This site, prepared by schoolchildren, offers interesting information on igloos, tepees, and other types of houses.

Houses of the Future (www.thinkquest.org/library/site_sum. html?lib_id=6328&team_id=CR0213643). This student-written site looks at the features that might be included in the house of the future.

How House Construction Works (www.howstuffworks. com/house.htm).This Web site includes in-depth information about how houses are built and the many details of what goes into home construction.

Roman Art and Architecture (http://harpy.uccs.edu/roman). Roman construction, design, and the empire's famous buildings are described at this Web site.

Index